A CENTURY OF
BROMLEY

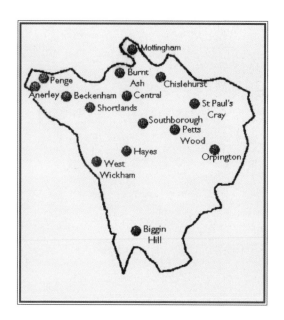

Market Square, Bromley, *c.* 1920.

A CENTURY OF
BROMLEY

DAVID JOHNSON

SUTTON PUBLISHING

First published in 1999 by Sutton Publishing Limited

This new paperback edition first published in 2007 by
Sutton Publishing, an imprint of NPI Media Group
Cirencester Road · Chalford · Stroud · Gloucestershire · GL6 8PE

British Library Cataloguing in Publication Data
A catalogue record for this book is available from the British Library.

ISBN 978-0-7509-4927-9

Front endpaper: Market Square, Bromley, *c.* 1918. On the left is the Food Office and to the right is Marks &
Spencer's Penny Bazaar.
Back endpaper: The Mayor, 1997–8, Councillor Mrs I.A. Buckley, with Bromley Councillors and guests,
including, to the Mayor's left, the Mayor of Bromley's Rhineland twin town Neuwied, Manfred Scherrer. Mayor
Scherrer was visiting in 1997 to celebrate the tenth year of twinning. The Civic Centre is in the background.
Half title page: Diagrammatical map of the Borough of Bromley.
Title page: St Mary Cray Fair, 1983.

Typeset in Photina.
Typesetting and origination by
Sutton Publishing.
Printed and bound in England.

Contents

BRITAIN: A CENTURY OF CHANGE   7
    Roger Hudson

BROMLEY: AN INTRODUCTION   15

BEFORE THE FIRST WORLD WAR   19

'IT WILL ALL BE OVER BY CHRISTMAS'   35

BRAVE NEW WORLD   49

THE SECOND WORLD WAR   65

'YOU'VE NEVER HAD IT SO GOOD'   79

THE SEVENTIES AND EIGHTIES   93

THE END OF THE CENTURY   107

ACKNOWLEDGEMENTS AND PICTURE CREDITS   121

The Queen visited to open the new Council Chamber at Bromley Civic Centre in 1986. She brought sunshine in her walkabout: 'We have visited London's cleanest and greenest borough', she said.

Britain: A Century of Change

Churchill in RAF uniform giving his famous victory sign, 1948.
(Illustrated London News)

The sixty years ending in 1900 were a period of huge trans-
formation for Britain. Railway stations, post-and-telegraph
offices, police and fire stations, gasworks and gasometers, new
livestock markets and covered markets, schools, churches, football
grounds, hospitals and asylums, water pumping stations and sewerage
plants totally altered the urban scene, and the country's population
tripled with more than seven out of ten people being born in or moving
to the towns. The century that followed, leading up to the Millennium's
end in 2000, was to be a period of even greater change.

When Queen Victoria died in 1901, she was measured for her
coffin by her grandson Kaiser Wilhelm, the London prostitutes put on
black mourning and the blinds came down in the villas and terraces
spreading out from the old town centres. These centres were reachable
by train and tram, by the new bicycles and still newer motor cars,
were connected by the new telephone, and lit by gas or even electricity.
The shops may have been full of British-made cotton and woollen
clothing but the grocers and butchers were selling cheap Danish bacon,
Argentinian beef, Australasian mutton and tinned or dried fish and fruit
from Canada, California and South Africa. Most of these goods were
carried in British-built-and-crewed ships burning Welsh steam coal.

King Edward VII receiving
'addresses of welcome'
at the Guildhall,
Gloucester, June 1909.
(Sutton collection)

As the first decade moved on, the Open Spaces Act meant more parks, bowling greens and cricket pitches. The First World War transformed the place of women, as they took over many men's jobs. Its other legacies were the war memorials which joined the statues of Victorian worthies in main squares round the land. After 1918 death duties and higher taxation bit hard, and a quarter of England changed hands in the space of only a few years.

Crowds celebrate Armistice Day outside Buckingham Palace as the royal family appears on the balcony, 1918. *(Illustrated London News)*

The multiple shop – the chain store – appeared in the high street: Marks & Spencer, Sainsburys, Maypole, Lipton's, Home & Colonial, the Fifty Shilling Tailor, Burton, Boots, W.H. Smith. The shopper was spoilt for choice, attracted by the brash fascias and advertising hoardings for national brands like Bovril, Pears Soap, and Ovaltine. Many new buildings began to be seen, such as garages, motor showrooms, picture palaces (cinemas), 'palais de dance', and ribbons of 'semis' stretched along the roads and new bypasses and onto the new estates nudging the green belts.

During the 1920s cars became more reliable and sophisticated as well as commonplace, with developments like the electric self-starter making them easier for women to drive. Who wanted to turn a crank handle in the new short skirt? This was, indeed, the electric age as much as the

motor era. Trolley buses, electric trams
and trains extended mass transport
and electric light replaced gas in the
street and the home, which itself was
groomed by the vacuum cleaner.

A major jolt to the march onward
and upward was administered by the
Great Depression of the early 1930s.
The older British industries – textiles,
shipbuilding, iron, steel, coal – were
already under pressure from foreign
competition when this worldwide slump arrived. Luckily there were new
diversions to alleviate the misery. The 'talkies' arrived in the cinemas;
more and more radios and gramophones were to be found in people's
homes; there were new women's magazines, with fashion, cookery tips
and problem pages; football pools; the flying feats of women pilots like
Amy Johnson; the Loch Ness Monster; cheap chocolate and the drama
of Edward VIII's abdication.

Houghton of Aston Villa
beats goalkeeper Crawford
of Blackburn to score the
second of four goals, 1930s.
(Illustrated London News)

Things were looking up again by 1936
and new light industry was booming in the
Home Counties as factories struggled to keep
up with the demand for radios, radiograms,
cars and electronic goods, including the
first television sets. The threat from Hitler's
Germany meant rearmament, particularly of
the airforce, which stimulated aircraft and
aero engine firms. If you were lucky and
lived in the south, there was good money to
be earned. A semi-detached house cost £450,
a Morris Cowley £150. People may have
smoked like chimneys but life expectancy,
since 1918, was up by 15 years while the
birth rate had almost halved.

In some ways it is the little memories that
seem to linger longest from the Second World
War: the kerbs painted white to show up in
the blackout, the rattle of ack-ack shrapnel on
roof tiles, sparrows killed by bomb blast. The
biggest damage, apart from London, was in the
south-west (Plymouth, Bristol) and the Midlands (Coventry, Birmingham).
Postwar reconstruction was rooted in the Beveridge Report which set
out the expectations for the Welfare State. This, together with the
nationalisation of the Bank of England, coal, gas, electricity and the
railways, formed the programme of the Labour government in 1945.

WAAF personnel tracing
the movement of flying
bombs and Allied fighters
on a plotting table, 1944.
(Illustrated London News)

British soldiers taking part
in an anti-gas drill, 1939.
(Illustrated London News)

Times were hard in the late 1940s, with rationing even more
stringent than during the war. Yet this was, as has been said, 'an
innocent and well-behaved era'. The first let-up came in 1951 with
the Festival of Britain and there was another fillip in 1953 from the
Coronation, which incidentally gave a huge boost to the spread of TV.
By 1954 leisure motoring had been resumed but the Comet – Britain's
best hope for taking on the American aviation industry – suffered a series

of mysterious crashes. The Suez debacle of 1956 was followed by an acceleration in the withdrawal from Empire, which had begun in 1947 with the Independence of India. Consumerism was truly born with the advent of commercial TV and most homes soon boasted washing machines, fridges, electric irons and fires.

A police radio controller at Scotland Yard, 1947. *(Illustrated London News)*

The *Lady Chatterley* obscenity trial in 1960 was something of a straw in the wind for what was to follow in that decade. A collective loss of inhibition seemed to sweep the land, as the Beatles and the Rolling Stones transformed popular music, and retailing, cinema and the theatre were revolutionised. Designers, hairdressers, photo-graphers and models moved into places vacated by an Establishment put to flight by the new breed of satirists spawned by *Beyond the Fringe* and *Private Eye*.

In the 1970s Britain seems to have suffered a prolonged hangover after the excesses of the previous decade. Ulster, inflation and union troubles were not made up for by entry into the EEC, North Sea Oil, Women's Lib or, indeed, Punk Rock. Mrs Thatcher applied the corrective in the 1980s, as the country moved over more and more from its old manufacturing base to providing services, consulting, advertising, and expertise in the 'invisible' market of high finance or in IT.

The post-1945 townscape has seen changes to match those in the worlds of work, entertainment and politics. In 1952 the Clean Air Act served notice on smogs and pea-souper fogs, smuts and blackened buildings, forcing people to stop burning coal and go over to smokeless sources of heat and energy. In the same decade some of the best urban building took place in the 'new towns' like Basildon, Crawley, Stevenage and Harlow. Elsewhere open warfare was declared on slums and what was labelled inadequate, cramped, back-to-back, two-up, two-down, housing. The new 'machine for living in' was a flat in a high-rise block. The architects and planners who promoted these were in league with the traffic engineers, determined to keep the motor car moving whatever the price in multi-storey car parks, meters, traffic wardens and ring roads. The old pollutant, coal smoke, was replaced by petrol and diesel exhaust, and traffic noise.

Fast food was no longer only a pork pie in a pub or fish-and-chips. There were Indian curry houses, Chinese take-aways and American-style hamburgers, while the drinker could get away from beer in a wine bar. Under the impact of television the big Gaumonts and Odeons closed or were rebuilt as multi-screen cinemas, while the palais de dance gave way to discos and clubs.

From the late 1960s the introduction of listed buildings and conservation areas, together with the growth of preservation societies, put a brake on 'comprehensive redevelopment'. The end of the century and the start of the Third Millennium saw new challenges to the health of towns and the wellbeing of the nine out of ten people who now live urban lives. The fight is on to prevent town centres from dying, as patterns of housing and shopping change, and edge-of-town supermarkets exercise the attractions of one-stop shopping. But as banks and department stores close, following the haberdashers, greengrocers, butchers and ironmongers, there are signs of new growth such as farmers' markets, and corner stores acting as pick-up points where customers collect shopping ordered on-line from web sites.

Futurologists tell us that we are in stage two of the consumer revolution: a shift from mass consumption to mass customisation driven by a desire to have things that fit us and our particular lifestyle exactly, and for better service. This must offer hope for small city-centre shop premises, as must the continued attraction of physical shopping, browsing and being part of a crowd: in a word, 'shoppertainment'. Another hopeful trend for towns is the growth in the number of young people postponing marriage and looking to live independently, alone, where there is a buzz, in 'swinging single cities'. Theirs is a 'flats-and-

Manchester during the
Commonwealth Games
in 2002. The city, like
others all over the country,
has experienced massive
redevelopment and
rejuvenation in recent years.
(Chris Makepeace)

cafés' lifestyle, in contrast to the 'family suburbs', and certainly fits in
with government's aim of building 60 per cent of the huge amount of
new housing needed on 'brown' sites, recycled urban land. There looks
to be plenty of life in the British town yet.

Bromley: An Introduction

According to the census of 1901 the population of the district, now known as the London Borough of Bromley, stood at just over 100,000. Three-quarters of that population lived in Beckenham, Bromley and Penge. From these towns a large proportion of the employed people commuted daily to central London, especially the City of London. To the south places like West Wickham and Hayes were villages surrounded by wood and farmland.

People chose to live in the Bromley area for a number of reasons, including good train services, the attraction of nearby rural areas, parks, sports, churches and access to entertainment. The leafy suburbs now stretch to the villages of a century ago, such as West Wickham. Electrification of the railway services in the mid-1920s helped to hasten development. Orpington to the south-east is also now urbanised. It had a population of just over 4,000 in 1901 and was then famous for its Orpington breeds of chicken.

The Borough is still largely a dormitory area for central London, and the 2001 census showed that 295,532 people were living in Bromley.

Beckenham High Street, *c.* 1930. Between the vehicles is the original Sainsbury's store.

The Borough with nearly 60 square miles is the largest, in terms of land area, of the London boroughs.

The individual towns and villages of the Borough were mostly within the Bromley Poor Law Union from 1836 to 1930. There was therefore an historical precedent for the area which formed the Borough established in 1965. Penge, in Surrey, was in the Croydon Poor Law Union in 1900. Penge then decided to become part of Kent and subsequently, in 1965 it was included in the London Borough of Bromley. Less than 6 miles from the City of London, Penge Hill today supports the dominating BBC TV aerial. The hill is 365 ft high and the aerial tower 728 ft so that it reaches well over 1,000 ft above sea level. Visible for miles, the tower is a poignant reminder of the Crystal Palace which stood here from 1854 to 1936. The Palace site and grounds are now wholly within the London Borough of Bromley, providing 200 acres of parkland. The Crystal Palace Sports Centre provides facilities to international standard.

At the southern end of Bromley, over 16 miles from the City, the beautiful North Downs are over 700 ft in height. The Downland area to the south and south-east of the Borough today has attractive villages like Cudham, Downe and Chelsfield. In parts these villages retain the appearance they had in 1900, and earlier. They are predominantly surrounded by prosperous farmland, as they were in 1900, and still provide attractive country walks. Biggin Hill, or Aperfield as it was once called, was also rural. The Royal Flying Corps (RFC) established

High Street, Orpington, *c.* 1949.

16

a station here in 1916 and the RAF continued occupation from 1918. They were ready to fight the Battle of Britain in 1940 – but the airfield and surrounding houses were badly damaged. Now, with the departure of the RAF in 1992, we have a wholly civil airport.

Mottingham is the northernmost part of the Borough, less than 4 miles from the Thames at Greenwich. The London County Council built the Mottingham Estate between the wars and after 1945. Eltham College, its playing fields and some of the old village have not changed in appearance much since 1900. W.G. Grace, the great cricketer, lived at Fairmount from 1909 to 1915. Another sporting hero, Eric Liddell, was a pupil at Eltham College. It is good to think that he trained here and went on to win a gold medal for the 400 metres in the Olympic Games of 1924. The film *Chariots of Fire* showed his sporting and religious zeal.

H.G. Wells, born in Bromley, based some of his books on his early years here. The atmosphere of the early part of the twentieth century can be visualised – people like him were happy to cycle into the nearby country to clear 'the cobwebs from the brain' . . . and 'return to your work really refreshed'. Richmal Crompton also lived in the Borough and the '20s and '30s can be glimpsed in the middle-class settings of her 'William' stories. The amusing William pranks are set in large houses with domestic help, and are easily imagined. Many such large houses still exist in Bromley.

The Glades, Bromley, under construction, 1980s.

West Wickham High Street, *c.* 1990.

In the First World War Bromley provided many hospitals. Some were purpose built, such as at Orpington; others were buildings adapted for the purpose. Church halls, schools and even private houses provided beds for the wounded. Two newly built schools in Beckenham, Cator and Balgowan, first served as hospitals. The nursing staff were often local ladies who volunteered. The Red Cross and St John Ambulance were much in evidence in Bromley, which was one of the first places in which the wounded were treated.

The interwar years were mainly prosperous in this corner of the suburbs, although there were also unemployed people, and their rehabilitation from the Depression was a local concern. However, the vast expansion of housing estates in the 1930s helped to ease unemployment. West Wickham, Orpington, Beckenham and Bromley lost their fields to provide good housing.

The Second World War was a struggle for the civilians as well as for those who joined the Armed Services. The bombing lasted five years and stretched the Civil Defence to the utmost. It was difficult to complete a full week's work and also be a firefighter, work in hospitals or perhaps be a member of the Home Guard. Many lost their homes and loved ones. The author knows of one 'prisoner of war' father who, on his return after the war, found his wife and children had been killed.

The last half century has seen the change to happier and more prosperous times and a major development in our local government. The communities of Beckenham, Bromley, Chislehurst, Orpington, Penge, West Wickham and rural areas were fused in 1965 to form the present Borough. The Borough is forward- and outward-looking. We have a link with our German twin town, Neuwied, and our position near to the Continent gives optimism for business expansion.

Before the
First World War

On 8 May 1900, Mafeking Day, celebrations at Chislehurst took the form
of a parade. This young lady is dressed in good fashionable clothing of
the time. Cycle ownership then was a display of status greater than car
ownership today. The cycle is very well decorated with a picture of the
Mafeking hero included in the patriotic spectacle.

Orpington hop pickers, 1900. The local people all helped to gather in the harvest of Kent hops. Schoolchildren were given a holiday so they could help this part of the local economy. Everyone seems overdressed and all wear hats.

Everard Alexander Hambro, of Hambro's Bank, owned a number of early motors. This one is outside Hayes Place and is chauffeur driven. Hayes Place was once owned by Prime Minister William Pitt. A later building with the same name was owned by E.A. Hambro from 1880 until 1925 when he died. The son, Charles, sold Hayes Place for housing development. Some of the 35 roads that now stand on the estate created are named after the former well-known owners of Hayes Place.

Chislehurst Caves, 1900. These caves are a tourist attraction, helped by the nearness of Chislehurst railway station. The Priest's Altar is shown in the part called the Inner Workings or Druid's. It all makes for a good day out.

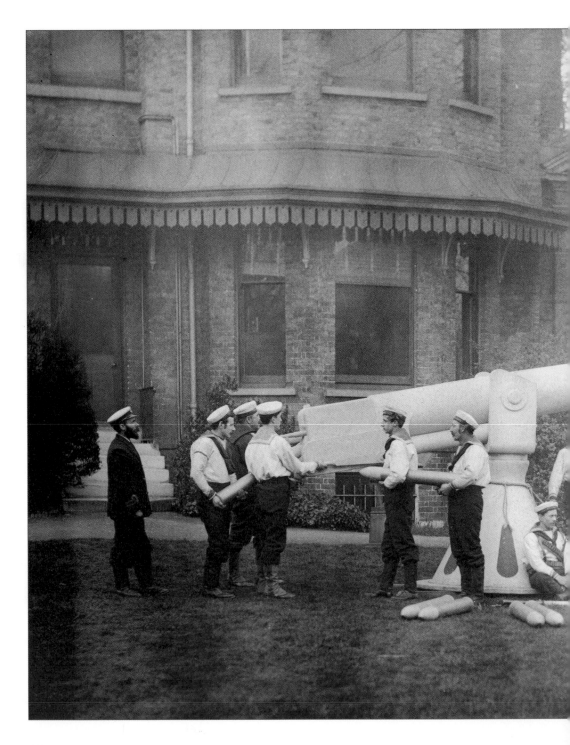

The gun, 1900. People at this time were concerned with the war in South Africa. This full-scale model of a naval gun was on display to raise funds for the war. It is shown in Beckenham Road, now High Street, Penge.

The technology of 1900 shown here is a steam traction elevator. The picture was taken within the area of the present housing estate around Bourne Vale, Hayes. Steam engines were still in use on farms into the 1940s. Oil-driven tractors were available from 1899 and by the 1940s had mostly replaced the cart-horses depicted here. In the previous century 'Swing riots' at Orpington and other places had greeted the introduction of mechanisation, people fearing the loss of their livelihoods.

Looking up the Bromley High Street from near the present day W.H. Smith's, 1900. The 'White Hart Inn and Posting House' is to the right. This served, as other inns did, for all types of meetings, until the Town Hall replaced it. The original Town Hall, in the centre of the picture, was demolished in 1932. The background chimney is part of Bromley's electrical works, built in 1898.

The first English airship, 1902. This is the first dirigible in this country, flown at the Crystal Palace by Stanley Spencer. It was tethered on 23 June, and on 19 September it was steered over the Borough. There are still people locally who can remember watching, from a distance, daring young men fly from the Palace grounds in the first quarter of the twentieth century.

The Queen's Garden, *c.* 1902. This was opened in 1900 'to commemorate the illustrious reign of Her Majesty Queen Victoria'. The space was previously the White Hart cricket field. The building is the Homoeopathic Hospital. Damaged in the Second World War, it was demolished in 1959. In the foreground Edwardian fashions, especially the hats, are displayed where today people take their lunch.

Wickham Hall stables, 1903. The expensive and large stables were owned by the Mellin family who made baby food. The buildings now serve Marks & Spencer

Charter Day procession, September 1903. Glorious sunshine welcomed the Bromley Mayor as well as the trumpeters of the Royal Horse Artillery, Bromley Volunteer's band and the fire brigade with their engine. Bromley had been an Urban District and now had Borough status. The coach is in Beckenham Lane, Shortlands.

The staff of St John's School, Penge, 1903. This National Church of England school took pupils from around the Borough and outside. When obtaining a scholarship to a secondary school was all important, this school always did well. Pupils often got office jobs in the City directly from the school. The smart turn-out of the teachers and headmaster reflects its high reputation.

The view from Bromley Market Square, *c.* 1905, shows that the parish church stood nearer the road than today. The bombed church was rebuilt to give more space to the north of the church. 'The Partridge' now stands behind the little girl and this view still provides a scene reminiscent of the country market town that was once Bromley.

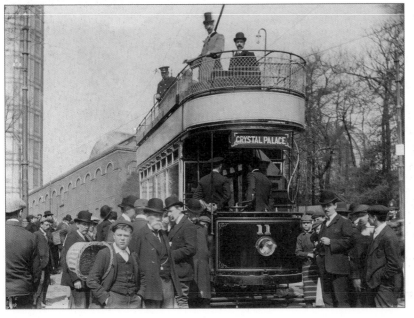

Inspection of the tram service, April 1906. The first tram link with Croydon from the Borough was to Anerley and Penge. The dignity of the official wearing the top hat contrasts with the errand boys on Anerley Hill. Poor children worked full-time from the age of twelve years at that time. The 284 ft high Brunel South Tower can be seen in the background. The trams also ran through Penge to Thicket Road.

Orpington's new
fire station, 1908.
The Chislehurst Road fire
station was opened on
26 November with local
people to cheer the
occasion. The crowd all
wore hats and the ladies'
hats are very elaborate.

Mechanised army battling to Hastings, 17 March 1909. The Brigade of Guards are the passengers passing The Plough on
Bromley Common. The exercise was called 'The Relief of Hastings' and took place to make sure the coast could be reached
quickly by mobile defenders. This was forward thinking, possibly as a result of the lessons learnt in the Boer War.

Penge Council inspection of a
fire engine, 1909. The inspection
at the Crystal Palace of the
Merryweathers Patent Petrol Fire
Engine illustrates the arrival of
the mechanised age.

In 1909 Baden Powell held the first large gathering of Boy Scouts in the Crystal Palace grounds. Imagine his surprise to find Girl Scouts asking to join. People in the local Boy Scout organisations were ahead of their time, since at their first meeting in 1909 they amended the proposed local rules to include troops of Girl Scouts. Baden Powell decided on a separate organisation for girls and they became Girl Guides from 1910. The girl standing was from Beckenham, which claims the oldest Girl Guide Company.

Anchor and Hope, Orpington, 1910. This High Street inn was built in the seventeenth century. Orpington expanded during the first decades of the twentieth century and modern buildings became fashionable. The old inn was rebuilt in 1929.

Empire Day, girls of Annunciation School, Chislehurst, 1911. Empire Day was 24 May: many schoolchildren attended celebrations and were given a half day off school. This ceremony continued until 1939. The Annunciation Girls' School was bomb-damaged in the Second World War and the building closed. Sainsbury's now stands on the site.

Chislehurst Flower Show, 1912. Flower shows were held in Beckenham, Bromley and many other places around the Borough. This show is at Rectory Meadow and the Rector, Canon J.E. Dawson, is in the foreground. Walnut Tree Close now stands here.

Farnborough, 1913. Fine weather on an Easter Monday has almost caused traffic congestion along the road to Hastings. The 47 bus was a popular route to the country at Farnborough for Bromley people. The bus could have been travelling to the Front the following year.

Keston Ponds Swimming Club, 1913. The Caesar's Well spring water of the ponds is normally cold but these Spartan swimmers enjoyed their morning exercise. Swimming is no longer allowed, but older people will remember swimmers here until at least 1939. The diving platform posts were just visible in 1999.

This clothing shop in Bromley Market Square, seen here in 1913, was owned by Alfred Strachan. The clothing does not look up-market like Skinner and Grant, a nearby competitor. The pawnbrokers were also near and they would undercut with second-hand clothing. The mature-looking assistant is Sidney Palmer, seventeen years of age. One wonders just what happened to him in the war to come.

Hayes post office staff, 1913. The bearded gentleman behind the ladies is Robert Pearce, Postmaster. He delivered letters until he was eighty-one years old. The sorting office and St Mary's Cottages around the post office were built by the merchant banker E.A. Hambro of Hayes Place. The rich benefactors of this time were soon to disappear.

'It will all be over by Christmas'

Bugle Boy, 1915. This Congregational Church Boy Scout,
immaculatelyturned out, is blowing the 'All Clear'.
The warning of an attack was given by firing maroons at the fire station.
Scouts cycled round the streets blowing their bugles after a raid, which
was a welcome sound.

Ambulance training, 1913. First Aid training started well before the war. It was all very thorough and some air raids and civilian casualties seem to have been expected. The exercise included collecting simulated casualties, with labels to show their injuries, from Hayes Common. Red Cross and St John Ambulance finally treated the 'injured' at Masons Hill School.

YMCA Scouts, 1914. The Scoutmaster, George Johnson, is the fifth person from the left, second row. He did his patriotic duty and joined the army, serving as a sergeant. He was injured in the war. Others in the group also served. This group has changed its name but at this time it was the 1st Penge YMCA. It has a continuous history from the start of Scouting. This is also the case with at least one other Borough Group, the 3rd Bromley.

Troops in Chislehurst, 13 August 1914. The Borough was on the direct path to the Channel ports and soldiers were frequently seen, as in this case, on the way to Dover at the start of the war. The weather is sunny; everyone was optimistic. These soldiers are regulars, part of the British Expeditionary Force, but others enrolled quickly so that they would be in the war that would be over by Christmas.

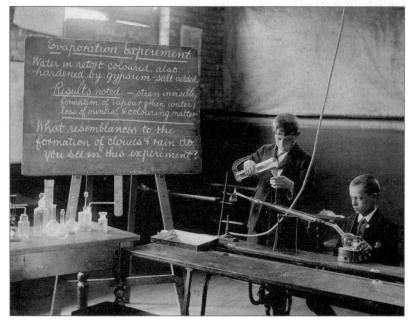

Chislehurst Road School, Orpington, 1914. Many Borough schools had provision for children above the compulsory age of attendance, which was twelve. The curriculum was expanded in the 'Elementary' schools as instanced in this science lesson. Readers who are old enough will be able to recall the smell of the chalk and use of a blackboard. Free school meals for poorer children were provided from 1914.

Wounded at Bromley station, 1914.
The soldiers were given refreshments
as soon as they arrived on the Bromley
platform. The local people provided this as
very willing volunteers.

The wounded were then conveyed to
hospitals, which were often church halls.
Private houses were also used. Mr Coles
gave up part of his home, Bromley Palace,
now Civic Centre. Mostly this work was
done by volunteers in their own private
cars.

Beckenham Secondary School building
opened on 4 June 1901. This distinctive
and attractive building appears to have
no role in 2007. This unique beacon of
municipal secondary learning, probably
a first in England, needs use and care.
From 1914 better provision was made
for child welfare. This is one of the
first Local Authority schools to provide
secondary education. By an Act of 1918
more than a quarter of local pupils would
be given free places on a competitive basis
at such schools.

Kelsey Manor, Beckenham, June 1915. Red Cross staff entertain their patients on the lawns of Kelsey Manor, now the beautiful Kelsey Park. Robin Hood and Friar Tuck fight quarterstaff – not too lethal.

Inter-Hospital Sports at Beckenham Cricket Ground between patients and staff of Christ Church and Balgowan Red Cross hospitals, 1915. Christ Church Hospital later included the large school built as Beckenham Girls' Secondary or Grammar School.

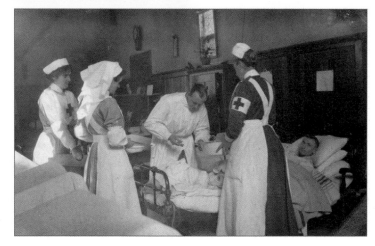

Christ Church Hospital, Beckenham, 1915. This scene is in the lower hall of the church halls. Dr Strickland is changing a dressing, assisted by Sister Savoy and Red Cross staff.

Balgowan School, 1915. This is the motorised ambulance section of Kent 41 – Men's Detachment. Children in the twenty-first century are informed about the school's use as a hospital.

Balloons inflated for fun, 1915. The sports obstacle race included blowing up a balloon, which could not have been easy for these wounded soldiers. Local people organised this event in the well-known Beckenham Cricket Ground.

Chislehurst Volunteers relax on the parched grass in the sun, Sunday 1 August 1915. This contrasts with the mud in which many would later die. Seated in the front row, fifth from the left, is their Commander, Captain L.J. Jackson.

Military Hospital, Orpington, 1916. Canadians played a big part in the war and the Province of Ontario representatives decided t site their hospital in Orpington because the area 'was most charming and healthful'. It was originally planned as a temporary reception hospital for wounded. It was opened by the Secretary of State for the Colonies, Bonar Law, on 16 February 1916.

In 1916 women felt they had to do their bit to help the lads at the front. This picture was taken inside spacious Oakley House, which is still with us. The Bromley Corps of the Kent Voluntary Aid Detachment (VAD) are rolling bandages and making slippers for wounded soldiers. The articles prepared were sent to a depot at Elsternwick, in Plaistow Lane, which supplied the whole of Kent with such items.

Christmas in St Mary's, 1916. St Mary's Church Hall was used as a VAD hospital and the soldiers expressed their gratitude: 'What splendid work the ladies of Bromley are doing.' At least one soldier has entered into the fun by wearing a nurse's head covering.

The 7th London Regiment, Green Street Green, 1917. To be billeted in a brewery would be many soldiers' dream. They are indeed using the Fox and Sons Brewery as a barracks, but it had closed in 1909!

43

Above: Labour Shortage, 1918. Labour shortages worsened as the war progressed. Women took on men's jobs or young boys were employed. Here a young lad delivers milk in churns, the normal method before milk bottles.

The kitchens of Cator Park School, Lennard Road, 1918. The school buildings were designated Christ Church Hospital. The secondary schoolgirls were and still are made aware of the first use for their building.

Band at Ontario Military Hospital, 1918. Entertainment was provided for the wounded in an effort to keep their spirits high. The band is packing to go. The Canadian Government paid for the hospital's maintenance: it treated over 12,000 Canadian soldiers and over 3,000 from other countries.

Tilling Buses at Farnborough, 1918. Similar buses were used to carry troops to the front in France and Belgium. They went into service before the First World War and were withdrawn in the mid-'20s.

45

On 25 June 1919 a 'Home-coming Welcome' service was held in The Cockpit, Chislehurst Common. 'Hymns Ancient and Modern' were sung at the place where they were compiled, for Canon F.H. Murray with his curates organised the production of the well-known hymn book. He was earlier Rector of St Nicholas' Church, which dominates the scene.

Postwar YMCA Scouts. The story of the Scoutmaster shows sadness and the appreciation which people in Bromley felt towards servicemen. Here, fourth from the left in the third row, George Johnson now looks depressed. The man in the white collar, Bernard Stewart, was a boy at the start of the war and then served as a sergeant in the Army. He was known to thousands as a well-known local Scout Commissioner up to the 1960s.

ERECTED BY
PAST & PRESENT MEMBERS
OF THE
1ST PENGE Y.M.C.A. TROOP B.P. BOY SCOUTS
IN AFFECTIONATE MEMORY OF
SCOUT-MASTER C. A. JOHNSON,
"HE HELPED TO MAKE US MEN."

Monumental inscription to a Soldier, 1922. The picture tells the story. He suffered a nervous disorder as a result of war injuries and died. It was not counted as a war death but was caused by the war.

Brave New World

Queen Mary's visit to Farrington School, 30 June 1925. The purpose
of the visit was to open an extension to the school. The cloche hat and
other clothing are the height of fashion. Dorothy Pattinson and her
daughter Peggy, aged three years, are presented to the Queen.
Peggy wanted to know if the Queen liked her dress.

Children's Victory Ball, 1920. The ball was held in Beckenham Public Hall on 6 January. The hall is decorated with flags and banners which proclaim 'Victory! Rejoice and be glad.' It was reported in the *Journal* as the 'brightest merriest throng' that had been seen there for 'many a long day'.

In the 1920s and 1930s the Crystal Palace was still the largest centre of entertainment in the southern suburbs. It was the venue for football Cup Finals, a Royal Naval training establishment during the First World War and the War Museum after. Later a motor cycle dirt-track was constructed. The local residents did not want lighting at night and the noise involved, and the main local venue for this sport became a new track at New Cross. Dulwich can be seen beyond the Palace. The main building burned down in 1936.

The future king in Bromley, 1920. The United Services Club was honoured with a visit by the Duke of York, who at that time was not thought of as a future king. The Club was in London Road and was opened with funds from NAAFI. The Duke became king in 1936 and served the people of this country well, especially in the Second World War.

Orpington Hospital, Repair Shop, 1920. Many men were mentally affected by their war service and had to be kept in hospitals. This was one such home, in the care of the civil authorities. To aid their possible recovery, work was organised as shown here.

Orphans' party, 1921. The war left many local families fatherless. Voluntary organisations rallied round and gave support. The British Legion were very active in their concern, and this party demonstrates the efforts they made.

Above: Woodwork class, Orpington, 1922. Chislehurst
Road School had a skilled woodwork master,
Mr W. Marshall, who is at the back behind his pupils.
He made the Green Street Green war memorial.
This can be seen to his right.

Chelsfield bus, 1925. Transport improved steadily
after the war, opening up the hinterland of Bromley
as residential areas. Trains were electrified and along
with buses became more frequent. The 407 service
ran from Dartford, through the Crays, to Chelsfield,
from 1925 to 1934.

Above: Queen Mary at Founders' Day, Farrington School, 1925. The route to and from the Chislehurst school was lined with cheering crowds in Bromley and Bickley. Today Farrington School continues to offer a first-rate education for girls up to eighteen years and now also to boys up to eleven years old.

The Southlands Road Lido was opened by the Mayor of Bromley on 25 June 1925, when the Beckenham Ladies' and Beckenham Swimming Clubs entertained. Beckenham swimming clubs were strong during most of the twentieth century, producing a number of Olympic swimmers including Duncan Goodhew, the gold medallist. Three good indoor pools aided the training from 1939 to 1997. Sunny outdoor swimming pools, like Southlands, were thought to be very healthy in the 1920s and '30s. People would travel from all round the present Borough to use this lido in warm weather.

Tram works, Anerley, 1923. Tram lines need to be renewed from time to time so the residents of Bromley can expect this in the twenty-first century. Car and bus journeys from Beckenham to Croydon were a talking point before Tramlink, with claims of an hour for that journey of 5 miles. The jouney now takes 17 minutes by Tramlink.

Below: Steam train at Chelsfield, 1925. Steam locomotives hauled the long-distance services through the Borough up until the early 1960s. This short distance push-pull loco, working between Orpington and Sevenoaks, was withdrawn and scrapped in 1956.

Beating the Orpington Bounds, 1925. Each parish organised this event annually until maps made it unnecessary. Orpington had plenty of pleasant country for a fun 'beating'. This was the footpath from Towncourt Lane to Crofton Lane, much changed today. West Wickham and Hayes organised beating the bounds in the 1920s.

Chislehurst garden party, 1928. This Primrose League party is at Hawkwood. The dress length of the ladies on the left is in order of age – near ankle length for the older and mid-knee for the younger.

Bromley Chamber of Commerce garden party, *c.* 1930. This was held at the Skiltons' house in Westmoreland Road. The Bromley Chamber was founded in 1916 'to promote, advance and protect the general and commercial interest of the Borough'. In the 1960s they arranged shopping weeks and organised Christmas lights. Notice that the cloche hat has gone and the men all have well-cut suits with skilfully rolled lapels.

May Day celebrations, Melvin School, 1931. The fond mothers watch as the age-old country festival is danced by the girls. Much trouble was taken by the parents to buy and make up the special clothing. There was not a blade of grass to be seen in the school grounds, which were confined to a small yard. The Anerley girls made the best of their school and yard, which would be condemned if it existed today.

This 1933 garage at 1 Plaistow Lane advertises that it has high pressure washing plant, lubricating services, valeting services and cars for hire. With only two pumps there was a choice of two manufacturers of fuel.

National Provincial Bank, 194 High Street, Bromley, 1934. This building is now 'The Partridge', facing The Square. The old stucco interior is a delight. The scales were used for weighing coin, which included gold. No grilles stand between the customer and bank clerk.

Westminster Bank, 1936. The interior has grilles fitted, although only of moderate height. The same premises at 143 High Street, Bromley, are now a NatWest Bank. The interior today reflects the security needed in the twenty-first century,

The laying of the foundation stone of the enlarged West Wickham Lecture Hall. Miss Margaret MacAndrew performed the ceremony on 30 June 1934. When the Hall was opened on 20 October, by Sir Waldron Smithers MP, there was a celebration dance in the evening. Funds were raised for this rebuilding by local organisations.

West Wickham Flitch winners, Mr and Mrs Tom Smith, 1937. The Mothers' Union organised the first Annual West Wickham Fair and Flitch in connection with the Lecture Hall funds in 1934. The Flitch continued to be held outdoors until 1959; the last was held indoors in 1960. The Flitch was a fun trial. A married couple had to prove to the 'Judge', sporting a long wig, that they had lived in harmony for a year and a day. If, for example, a hostile witness claimed that the couple were at each other's throats, the couple would claim that the witness was hallucinating.

The view from the bottom of Masons Hill looking towards the west side of Bromley High Street, 1935. In the left foreground the hoardings read 'Ravensbourne Riding School' and 'Masons Hill Garage'. The next building is The Two Brewers. In the 1960s, '70s and '80s this was the site of Telephone House. Now the more tastefully designed Churchill Insurance Offices are here. The type ST 907 bus was in service from 1930 to 1947. David Greig's shop is on the right.

Holy Trinity, Beckenham, 1936. This is the Sunday School summer party held in the Vicar's garden. Most children at this time attended a church Sunday school with two treats a year. In the summer this was often an excursion to the seaside, or, like this one, paste and cucumber sandwiches, jelly, cakes and squash. The Christmas treat included a good present for every child. The author is second from the left and his brother is second from the right.

The man is walking past the old Five Bells with its smoky chimneys, c. 1937. The old pub is typical of buildings on Bromley Common and to the south, where local flints were utilised. The mock-Tudor style of the new building was perhaps at the height of fashion locally.

Coronation celebrations, 12 May 1937. This is the prize-winning float at Chislehurst. 'New Central School, Fab Opening, April 1st, 1987', is an interpretation of the main notice. A 1930s school class is depicted on the float.

Beckenham Hospital extension, 1939. On Tuesday 11 July HRH the Duchess of Gloucester opened the new part of the hospital. Josiah Stamp and the Matron are accompanying her. The hospital today has a number of out-patient clinics and is to be transmuted into Beckenham Beacon on completion of twenty-first century rebuilding. The dropping of the description hospital, with indeed a change of function, is not popular with many residents.

Winners of Beckenham Junior Cricket Cup, 1939. Alexandra School team were the proud winners. Mr Broadbent, the younger man, is the sports master, soon to serve in the RAF. The older man is Mr Dent, the headmaster, known as 'Daddy Dent' to the 'boys' and 'girls' who still enjoy a chat about those peaceful happy days.

The
Second World War

Winston Churchill visited Biggin Hill on 2 September 1939, the day before
war broke out. Greeting the young airmen, he said he had no doubts they
would be as brave as their forefathers in the coming conflict. Winston held
no office at this time. Prime Minister Chamberlain had asked him to be a
member of the War Cabinet the previous day.

Wardens' wedding, 1939. The Air Raid Precautions (ARP) organisation were ready for gas warfare as their anti-gas clothing shows. The fellow wardens of the happy couple, Mr and Mrs Tolhurst, formed a guard of honour dressed in their recently issued clothing.

Bromley ARP warden, 1940. Preparation for civil defence was thorough. The Bromley Borough organised talks which are advertised on the van. ARP posts were established in church halls and private houses. This one is at 42 Glenview Road, Bromley.

66

Chislehurst Heavy Rescue at Rose Cottage, Old Perry Street, 1940s. The squad are next to their specially adapted lorry. Members of one of the Beckenham ARP, Heavy Rescue squads were all killed at West Wickham by a flying bomb on 16 June 1944.

The Auxiliary Fire Service supported the regular Fire Service throughout the war. Many members were small businessmen who would work in their individual businesses in their time off duty. It was not a 'cushy number'; indeed many local men were killed. Here drill has been treated like a sport: Beckenham won and the runners-up are shown on the board. The names of the team, from top left, are: Clapp, Commandant Leeks, Forsyth, Biswell, Sayer, Masters and Oldfield.

Bombing, 1939–45. This is a scene typical
of the bombing, near Beckenham church.
Buildings were so devastated that it was
decided to leave the large bombed site as
open land; it is now called Beckenham
Green.

Gun on Hayes Common, 1940. Guns bristled around the Borough. Hayes guns were for a time manned by Canadians who took home thirty-four Hayes brides. The Vancouver Islanders have returned on visits, and one place they call on regularly is the Royal British Legion Club, Station Hill, Hayes.

Congregational church, Anerley, 1941. This church, like so many in the Borough, was 'blitzed'. The money received in compensation was used to build Hayes Free Church where new housing was in want of a good church.

Bromley parish church, 1941. The heaviest raid on Bromley was overnight, 16–17 April 1941. The parish church of St Peter and St Paul was destroyed, except for the tower. This was built into the reconstructed church standing today.

Above: On 27 May 1941 HRH Duke of Kent inspected 1,000 local Civil Defence personnel at Whitehall Recreation ground in Southlands Road. The Duke is talking to Chief Warden Proctor, and Admiral Sir Edward Evans is to the left. This was six weeks after Bromley's 'Big Raid' of 16–17 April. The Duke was killed on active service the following year, when the Sunderland aircraft carrying him crashed in Scotland.

Wartime transport, 1942. Incendiary bombs became a great menace in the mid-war years. This Borough ARP warden is equipped to reach trouble spots quickly. Notice that even a small lamp on a bicycle had to be masked so that it would be invisible to enemy aircraft.

On 6 March 1942 the CD parade is greeted outside the Bromley Municipal Offices by children and adults. A Naval band from Chatham has just marched by and coloured bunting lined the roads to greet the Regional Commissioner, Admiral Evans. Children watched many parades and patriotism was strong.

Beckenham Home Guard at Muirheads, 1943. The fifth man from the right front row is Ernie Kelley, the author's uncle. At the time of this photograph he kept a machine gun in his front porch, and was instructed to operate on his own to shoot enemy paratroopers. There is no doubt that he and many others meant to do this if invasion was attempted. The men are part of the 55th Battalion, which covered the Beckenham area. They were associated with London, but since they were in Kent they were also included as part of Kent Home Guard. They were affiliated to the Royal West Kent Regiment.

Boy Scouts, 1943. The scouts in this Borough supported the 'war effort' in many ways. They acted as messengers, collected waste paper, and dug out and erected shelters. Here Beckenham Scout Association parades through Penge High Street on the St George's Day Parade.

The 7th Beckenham, Lion Patrol at Summer Camp, 1943. Youth organisations often provided the only holiday at this time. The church these scouts were attached to was St Michael's, which was destroyed by fire bombs on 24 March 1944. Luckily the scout camping equipment was in an adjacent hut and miraculously survived.

Wartime concert party, 1943. Six of the
young men formed a band, thought to have
been the Dick Richards Dance Band, and
they played in halls all round the Borough.
A year later saw them all in uniform.
The young ladies seem a little over-dressed
by today's standards.

Air defences, Hayes. This is a range-
finder operated by 154th City of London
Regiment. Regular soldiers, British and
Canadian, as well as Home Guard members
defended Bromley. They suffered casualties
all over the Borough.

Ladies in uniform, 1944. These cheerful
ladies are members of the Coney Hall, West
Wickham, Auxiliary Fire Service. Many
men had already lost their lives in this
Service and their memorial can be seen at
West Wickham parish church.

Victory party, Bromley. This is the victory
party for the council estate of which
Hillside Road and Dykes Way were a part.
Hillside Road was badly damaged and the
1945 VE party is in Dykes Way.
Mr Draper (at the back) is standing by
his immaculately cut hedge.

Royal Observer Corps, 1945. Civilians manned observation posts to spot and track enemy aircraft. This is No. 19 Group 'C' at the end of the war. They could do nothing to help with V2 rockets, one of which caused the last civilian death in this country – at Orpington on 27 March 1945.

War damage, Shortlands, 1940s. Houses were often blasted rather than destroyed. The damage was normally repaired to allow habitation as soon as possible. This is Hillside Road near Dykes Way.

'You've never had it
so good'

Blackheath Harriers, House of Commons Dinner, 1959. The Hayes-based
Athletic Club held their annual dinner at the House, courtesy of their chief guest,
Prime Minister Harold Macmillan. He was MP for Bromley for twenty years.
To the PM's left, Vic Bearden is wearing his BHH Presidential badge.
A Beckenham resident, in his late nineties, he has stories to tell.
Their car carrying the Club's silver was stopped by Brixton Police when returning
in the small hours. An explanation for their unusual load was demanded.
The truth seemed far fetched to the policeman. 'That's a likely story, Sir,' was
the response. On checking, the police gave them and the precious trophies an
escort for the rest of the journey. Since 2003 this very successful club has been
called Blackheath & Bromley Harriers Athletic Club.

In October 1949 'thousands greeted a much-loved member of the Royal Family', 'Princess Charming lays foundation stone'. The *Bromley Mercury* continues: 'there was a wonderful display of colour in the streets and a real Kent welcome'. The old Bromley parish church was blitzed on the night of 16–17 April 1941; the dignitaries witnessed the start of the rebuilding. One little-known report by a workman on the site to the author was that they found no bodies in some eighteenth-century graves: body snatchers were suspected.

Traditional carol singing outside the White Hart, Christmas Eve, 1961. The Salvation Army Band leads the joyous celebrations just outside the old coaching inn, soon to be demolished. Littlewoods shop was constructed on the site in the 1960s and several other stores have occupied this site since then.

Richmal Crompton, Monday, 17 April 1950. Richmal Crompton autographed many of her William books at the opening of the new Junior Library, within the Central Library, Bromley. Her original surname was Lamburn, and she was a long-time resident of Bromley Common. (*Kentish Times*)

· ESTABLISHED IN 1887 ·

Ye olde Forge

· AD 1720 ·

BUILDING MATERIAL SUPPLY STORES

NETTLEFOLD'S
SCREWS BOLTS AND NUTS
ON SALE WITHIN

OILS
COLOURS
PAINTS
LEAD
PAPERHANGING
GLASS

Old forge, Croften Road, Locksbottom, 1950. Located near the Black Horse public house, the village forge by this time is an ironmonger's and supplies building material. This type of shop has virtually disappeared today.

Chislehurst village sign, 1953. This new sign depicts
Thomas Walsingham being knighted by Queen
Elizabeth I on the occasion of his marriage. He was
one of her courtiers, and lived at Scadbury Manor.

Below: Unveiling of Chislehurst village sign, 1953.
Members of the Marlowe Society are dressed in
Elizabethan costume for this ceremony. Thomas
Walsingham was a patron of Christopher Marlowe,
the poet. He was killed mysteriously at Deptford,
possibly by agents of Walsingham.

Mottingham Remembrance
Day service, 1954. The British
Legion organises many such
ceremonies. The Second World
War was fresh in people's minds
at this time and many present
knew someone who fell.

Above: Beckenham Amateur Cine Club, 1957. After the war prosperity allowed some to indulge in amateur film making. Ravensbourne station here makes a suitable Victorian backdrop.

Water tower, Summer Hill, Chislehurst, 1961. This tower was demolished in 1963 to the regret of many. At this time the 227 bus ran through this narrow arch. The road restrictions were too great for increasing traffic, so perhaps its demolition was essential.

The winter of 1962/3 was very severe. The snow lay for weeks, from Boxing Day to March. Ponds were frozen hard and there was no danger of falling through inches of ice; even running streams were frozen. Keston was among many ponds used for skating.

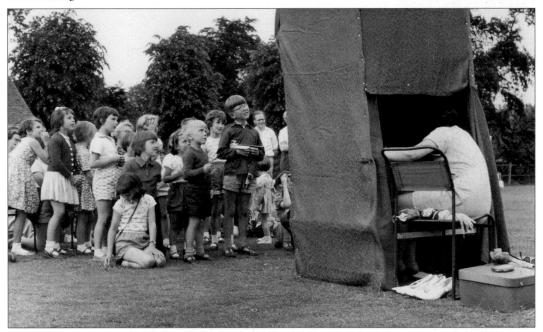

On 15 June 1963 Bromley Baptist Church children are being entertained by a student from Stockwell Teacher Training College. This College was the previous occupant of much of the building which is now the Bromley Civic Centre. The rapt attention of the children contrasts with the 'Wizard of Oz', working away to produce another world for the audience.

87

Crystal Palace Sports Centre, racing pool. The diving boards are above a separate deep diving pool. These are rare facilities, attracting athletes to the Borough for training. International events are held here. The Centre was opened by HRH Prince Philip on Monday 13 July 1964.

Bromley Baptist Church Sunday School centenary celebrations were held in 1964. The children are all smartly dressed for the occasion. Ralph Palfrey, a well-known local photographer, is the tallest person at the back. Leonard Fawkes is the Sunday School Superintendent standing in the centre and behind him is the Minister, John Gladstone.

In 1966 this small Tesco shop in Beckenham High street was a modest operation, with Green Shield stamps available. These were given in proportion to purchases and exchangeable for a wide range of goods other than food. In 1971 this shop was listed as a supermarket. It hardly compares with today's Elmers End massive Tesco store with petrol station. Beckenham Toys to the right, is one of the oldest stores in the town.

Flying saucer at Sundridge, September 1967. The picture evokes endless guesses about what the traffic warden said to the policemen or the other way round. 'Do you think they will have money for the fine?' The UFO was indeed loitering with intent, but not on a road and eventually no charges were made. Apprentices at RAF Farnborough, Hampshire, made six hoax flying saucers to publicise their rag week. This one was found early in the morning on Sundridge Park Golf Course by a surprised caddie. He reported its electronic noise to the police station, but a Scotland Yard explosives experts found only British batteries inside. (*Kentish Times*)

Temporary Central Library at Tweedy Road, 1968. The Carnegie Library in the High Street was demolished at this time to make way for the construction of the Churchill Theatre and new Central Library. The turn-of-the-century original library therefore had a new lease of life. The building has been converted into apartments in the twenty-first century.

Downe High Street, 1968. Downe had seven shops in 1900 and refreshment rooms. In 1968 a quiet village offered plenty of parking space. (*Kentish Times*)

Post office staff demonstration, Bromley, 1968. There were many labour disputes at this time and the Borough had its share. Counter clerks are outside the main Bromley office. (*Kentish Times*)

Post Office sorting office, Sherman Road, Bromley, 1969. Work practices were changing fast at this time and many workers became discontented. The pride of knowledge was of less value, as postal codes and sorting mechanisation replaced many of the forty-eight box fittings shown here. (*Kentish Times*)

Royal visit to Bromley, 15 May 1969. The Queen and Mayor leave the Old Town Hall. Princess Anne is in the background. The Princess sports a costume of the modern length, above the knee. (*Kentish Times*)

91

The Harrison and Gibson furniture store fire, February 1968. The store was on the west side of lower Bromley High Street. Heroism was shown by the manager, Mr Frederick Doe, in clearing each floor of shoppers while the building burnt. Firemen and policemen kept casualties to a minimum by their prompt action: only one casualty is recorded, and was not detained in hospital. When the roof collapsed 20 ft flames shot up and threatened firemen, who swung on their ladders to safety. (*Kentish Times*)

Flood of retribution, Sunday opening, 15 September 1968. The estate agents have a man with an umbrella at the door. They are open, but business is a wash-out. This is Beckenham High Street and is typical of Bromley's flooded roads. On the right of the picture is a glimpse of R. Tucker's shop; this was one of the last of the High Street's butchers. Nearby Tesco's store lost a quarter of its stock. The Ravensbourne and its tributaries overflowed causing many families to be marooned in upstairs rooms. The *Kentish Times* report that Homesdale Road and Queen Anne Avenue were flooded. Stevens' Garage in Bromley had been 'awash and Mrs Stevens' Sunday joint was water-logged in her cooker'.

The Seventies and Eighties

High Street buildings, St Mary Cray, early 1970s, possibly 1973. This area was bombed during the war and neglected for over twenty years. An Action Group was formed in 1971 by local residents concerned about the state of the village, especially ancient timber-framed buildings. Restoration work started in 1981.

St Mary Cary, 1970. Faith in this signpost was not strong. The mistake was, of course, just outside the Borough. The other side has the correct spelling of St Mary Cray.

Below: St Mary Cray summer fair, 1983. The Temple Boys' Brigade band marches past the fair stalls, which are to the right of the picture. All ages supported the St Mary Cray Action Group to raise funds. On this occasion it was funds to save the old coaching inn in the centre of the picture. This building was renamed Mary Rose.

The stall and bonny bonnets at the St Mary Cray Fair, 1983. All seem to be enjoying the fun, sporting summer clothes. Local residents, with faith in the future and pride in the past, are raising funds for village restoration work.

Mary Rose, 1980s. The building has now been fully restored. Notice the preservation of the large arched window, a relic of the former nineteenth-century Congregational chapel. The building is now a licensed restaurant called The Mary Rose. With an additional building it is now classed as an English Tourist Board Hotel category three. It has four-poster beds.

During the 1920s and 1930s local councils built houses and flats, like these, seen here in 1970. London County Council moved families from poorer housing to outside its borders. These flats were just in Bromley as part of the Downham Estate. They were bombed during the war, with fatalities. The rebuilt flats are now the happy setting for children at play long after the war.

The Mall, Bromley, 1970. This was the style of shopping when The Mall shopping precinct opened in September 1970. The car parking here was not very convenient and Sainsbury's moved to its present site, in West Street, where shoppers have better parking facilities. The Mall was partially rebuilt in 2004. (*Kentish Times*)

The Shaftesbury Society Coney Hill School, West Wickham, 1971. Miss Shirley Raymond, physiotherapist, serves with her shop. The school closed in 2005 and was replaced by another Christian teaching establishment, the Groom Shaftesbury, Nash College of Further Education. There are 65 residential and other students, all with severe special needs, aged between 19–25 years. The spina bifida children were helped to deal with their disabilities and trained for careers.

St Giles' Parish Centre, Farnborough, 13 April 1971. The Right Reverend H.D. Halsey, Bishop of Tonbridge, leads the dedication service in opening the centre. The Reverend David Webb, the Rector, is next to the Bishop. (*Kentish Times*)

Church Road, Bromley, 1972. Tetty Way and the old flintstone wall can be seen in the background. The Little Shop on the corner is about to be demolished along with the wall nearest the camera. This was formerly part of the famous Dr Scott's surgery. He brought much wealth to the town with his cures about 200 years ago.

Charles asks 'mind my bike', July 1972. HRH the Prince of Wales causes hilarity in Bromley. He was formally opening the newly built Churchill Theatre. (*Kentish Times*)

Closure of the Embassy at Petts Wood, 14 April 1973. *Snoopy Come Home* and *Mighty Mouse* were the last films shown here. Its first film was *A Tale Of Two Cities* on 12 October 1936. Closures of cinemas all round the Borough from the 1950s, until very recently, became more frequent as the popularity of television increased.

A bull in Bromley, 1979. Golden-Tip was the name of this magnificent bull held by the cowman, Bill Medlock, at Wickham Court Farm. The tenant farmer believed in traditional ways when most farmers chose to use artificial insemination. The farmer retired the following year and Golden-Tip was sold. Was this the last bull in Bromley?

Farm tool sale, 1980. Hedges were being damaged and livestock were becoming too difficult to keep on Wickham Court Farm by 1980. The old farmer retired and the new farmer planned to use modern methods. He also decided on less vulnerable farm produce. Change in agriculture locally has meant less livestock, except riding horses, which are more numerous than before.

Street party, West Wickham, 1981. The big wedding of the Prince and Princess of Wales is celebrated by the children of Birch Tree Avenue. The parents and grandparents would remember other street parties, which are an old tradition on great occasions.

Charles Darwin School, 1982. The schoolchildren seem to be very happy as they make their way home. Longer hair for the boys is fashionable. he school opened in 1973, and it was named after one of the most famous local residents, Charles Darwin, who lived and worked in Down House for forty years.

West Wickham Dairy, 1985. The stables which were part of the old Wickham Hall were at first used by United Dairies, and now continue as Marks & Spencer.

'Bromley At War' Library exhibition, December 1985. The exhibition included an indoor Morrison Shelter. Bromley Archivist, Miss E. Silverthorne, who retired mid-2007, is second from the right of the picture.

The Great Storm, 16 October 1987. This tree is next to a stone which records the planting to commemorate the Silver Jubilee of Elizabeth II. The wind caused widespread damage, closing many roads. The woodland footpaths still have fallen trees that cause diversions.

On 6 April 1989 smoke was seen around the roof of St George's Church, Bickley. The playgroup children were quickly evacuated from the church hall. Firefighters on arrival found the fire burning fiercely, and the church was badly damaged. The congregation reacted with spirit to raise funds and the building is now restored.

HRH the Queen visited Bromley on 26 March 1986 to a warm welcome on a cool day. The Queen was dressed in yellow, reflecting the spring flowers which were in their full glory in the Borough. Thousands cheered her car along the route to the Civic Centre. The roundabout, in front of the Baptist church, has gone: traffic lights now control the traffic to Kentish Way.

105

Bromley's first lady town crier. An 1989 advert was answered by this lady, Eunice Pearton, and she got the job. The suggestion to apply was from her family, who thought she had a loud voice! She 'cried' first to attract volunteers for charity work, and 'cried' in Penge and in many other parts of the Borough until 1996.

Pedestrianisation Day, Bromley, 29 July 1989.
The whole of the middle of Bromley High Street was reserved for pedestrians only from 1989. Shoppers can now enjoy their activities with greater safety.

The End of the Century

Dr Alexander Muirhead founded the Muirhead factory. Just before 1900
he moved his cable factory to Elmers End; he experimented with wireless
using an aerial at Downe. Muirhead's continued making
electro-mechanical equipment at Elmers End until the 1980s, when they
moved to Anerley where Aerospace components are now made.

The Glades and Scruffy Murphy's. The very large indoor shopping area was opened in October 1991 and has been very popular since. This is the Widmore Road entrance. The Three Compasses changed its name to Scruffy Murphy's. Now, after another change of fashion, it is called The Compass.

Below: A helicopter in the grounds of Charles Darwin School, Biggin Hill, 1993. This is one way to return to see your old school and teachers. Mick Eastwood was the newly qualified pilot who landed this large aircraft. The children were eager to see inside.

A visit by the Mayor to Chislehurst Caves, 1995. Councillor Priest and his wife chat with the author who, as a child, sheltered here during 1943 and 1944. Hundreds of people sought safety in the caves during the Second World War. There was virtually a town underground. This gathering was held to celebrate the fiftieth anniversary of peace.

In May 1996 the May Queen for Hayes Common, seated, was Sarah Clarke. Mr Deedy, a friend of John Ruskin, restarted the crowning of May Queen ceremonies in Greenwich Park at the turn of the twentieth century. Since 1914 London ceremonies have been held on Hayes Common, a place in the country at the end of the railway line.

The 'Neuwied' indicator in Bromley Market Square was added in 1997. This indicator is the only one that points to a place outside the Borough. The plate shows that our twin town in Germany is 350 miles away. The agreement to 'twin' was signed on the day of the Great Storm, 16 October 1987. From stormy times friendship has been developed.

Below: Eurostar train, Kent House, 1998. The Eurostar boarding stations are convenient enough to make day visits to France and Belgium a reasonable proposition.

Morris Men, before dawn on
1 May 1999. The Ravensbourne
Morris Men were welcoming
the dawn, near Caesar's
Well, Keston Common. The
organisation has raised money
for charities at many events over
the last fifty years.

Street market, Penge, 1999: the Mayor shopping in her regalia, perhaps. The Mayor had just opened two new Penge Squares.

ENGE
MAY
QUEEN
1999

The 1999 Penge May
Queen in happy times.
The ceremonies continued
during the Second World
War, despite the bombing.
Mothers every year still
work hard to dress their
children for this age-old
ceremony. Various parts
of the Borough are always
well represented and the
occasion appears to have a
good future.

113

Above: Christ Church, Beckenham, 1999. The girls' section of the choir is in front. The choir has had notable members, including Wesley Carr who later became Dean of Westminster Abbey and conducted the funeral of Diana, Princess of Wales. The choir, under their leader since 1955 Christian Strover, have won many competitions and scholarships.

H.G. Wells mural, Market Square, Bromley, 1980s. The novels of H.G. Wells were illustrated at the place of his early life. The foreground figures merged well with the mural, almost as though they were in the painting. A Darwin mural has replaced the one shown here.

Above: Muirhead's site, now a Tesco store, 1999. The large site left by Muirhead's, as well as other properties, now includes a fuel station. Note the 1999 price. With some exceptions, mainly Sunday nights, the store is open twenty-four hours a day.

The first tram ever at Beckenham, 15 August 1999.

Market day, Bromley, 1990s.
The Thursday markets are
still the place to get a good
bargain. Today picture
frames, hardware and
clothing are for sale. The
market is held by ancient
privilege, making Bromley a
market town.

Wet fish shop, Widmore Road, Bromley, 1999. Behind the fishmonger the entrance to The Glades is visible. Small shops still manage to compete with modern large stores, although this type of shop is now rare in the twenty-first century.

Civic Centre, Bromley, 1999. This was once the Palace used by the Bishops of Rochester. In succession it was a private residence, housed wounded soldiers in the First World War and was a college.

The former Roman road, Sparrows Den, West Wickham, during the dry summer of 1999. Grass roots above the road are unable to gain enough moisture, so this pale feature on the normally green field is an attraction in times of drought.

The Spa, Beckenham, 1999. The bright white walls give a clean appearance to The Spa. Swimmers are able to take a dip, most days, between 6.30 a.m. and 10 p.m. Improved hours are attracting swimmers from far and wide. Badminton, squash and other sports are also available.

Tessa Sanderson and the Mayor, Sue Polydorou, officially open The Spa, Beckenham, Saturday 17 July 1999. The Spa replaced the old swimming baths which were officially opened on 20 April 1901.

Acknowledgements and Picture Credits

My thanks are given to all those who offered pictures for inclusion in this book, even if I was not able to find space for every contribution.

Here I mention only those that are included in the book. The majority of the illustrations are from Bromley Library; remaining contributions are from:

V. Beardon, J. Blundell, K. Burtonshaw, Pat & June Bushell, A.J. Clark, The Copeland Collection (A.C. Johns), Farrington School, P.D. Gann, G.J. Hailey, J. Hilton, L.F. Johnson, Mrs Kelley-Stubbs, *Kentish Times*, the Peter Killick Collection, Mrs P. Knowlden, Mrs M. Konior, H. Leigh, Canon Lock, Bromley Parish Church, B. Morton, C. Pearton, C. Porteous, Porth Curno Ltd, A. Robinson, Miss M.I. Searle and Mrs Mudie, C. Stevens, Mrs C. Timms, Mrs J. Walker, John Watterson, D. Wood.

Mr R. Palfrey is thanked in particular for taking many recent pictures at my request.

Cudham Church from Berry's Hill – a scene of timeless beauty. (*Kentish Times*)